This book is presented to

_____

It was given to you by

_____

Date

_____

I love you

My BIG BOOK of Bible Stories

The Good Samaritan • The Pharisee and the Tax Collector • Nebuchadnezzar's Dream

Phil A. Smouse

In him was life,
and that life was the light of men.

John 1:4 NIV

My BIG BOOK of Bible Stories

VOLUME FIVE

In him was life, and that life was the light of men.
John 1:4 NIV

© 2011 by Phil A. Smouse
ISBN 9781790257591

"A walk," I thought. "Now, that sounds nice—
like paradise to be precise.
To Jericho. Yes, that will be
the thing to do today for me!"

But, oh my word, I never knew.
I never even had a clue
my jog-for-joy would turn into
a rendezvous with *you-know-who!*

You don't know who? Oh, sure you do.
I'll bet your Grandma knows him, too!

I strolled along. I sniffed the breeze.
Aaah, chamomile and peonies!
Yes, columbine and hollyhocks—
sweet lavender and creeping phlox.

Oh bliss! Oh joy! Oh, hybrid teas,
all borne upon the balmy breeze,
with honeysuckle—strawberries—
magnolia trees and. . .

STINKY CHEESE?

STINKY CHEESE!? Say what? Oh please!
Oh yes—the cheese that makes you *sneeze*.
Le-pew! Le-yuk! Le-hack! Le-wheeze!
Le-dirty, denim dungarees!

"Oh dear!" thought me. "What could it be?"
And then I spun around to see. . .

Two big, old, hairy, mean and scary
guys who any momentary
planned to take my happy day
and turn it 'round the other way!

They shook me up. They knocked me down.
They hauled me halfway back to town.
They snitched my clothes and snatched my cash.
They pulled and twisted my mustache.

Oh, Grandma told me not to go
down on the road to Jericho!

I tried to move, but nothing budged.
I'd been completely chocolate-fudged.
I needed help, to say the least.

That's when I saw the temple priest!

"Oh, icky poo. Now what is THAT
untidy mess?" the high-priest spat.

"That's really gross. How impolite,
to lay there right where I just might
be forced to look at such a sight.
Oh great, there goes my appetite."

And then with that, he took his feet,
and crossed them right across the street.

You're right. I should have been upset.
But listen, it's not over yet. . .

I heard the sound of soulful singing.
Psalms and hymns and tambo ringing.
Harps and zithers. Bells and whistles.
Holy rock and rolled epistles!

Man, I love that gospel sound!
That sound's the best dressed sound around.
And this guy, *he* could play it right.
THIS guy was really out of sight.

I guess he didn't see me there.
That must be why he didn't care
to stop and say, "How do you do?"
I would have stopped. Well, wouldn't *you?*

Of course you would. Of course you should.
Of course I fully understood,
that if you could you surely would,
but that won't do ME any good!

Who's *THAT,* you say? Who's *who?* Who's where?
OH NO! NOT THAT GUY OVER THERE!

When THAT guy gets a hold of me,
I'll be as boo-booed as can be!
I tell you, there has NEVER been
a truly good Samaritan.

Oh yes, I know. I'm so ashamed!
I never, *ever* should have blamed
that precious, tender, gentle man—
that godly, good Samaritan.

He patched up all my lumps and thumps.
He *bandaged* all my boo-boo bumps.
He rode me back on into town,
then picked me up and set me down—

yes, set me down without a sound
right in the best hotel around!

This cannot be! Not HIM— not ME.
This man's as puzzling as can be.

But he was warm, and true, and real.
He told me Jesus Christ could *heal*
my busted, broken, banged up heart. . .

So I said *yes*, it's time to start.

Two men went to church one day.
They went to church so they could pray.
Two men as different as can be—
the tax-man and the Pharisee.

The *Phari-who?* The Pharisee!
And who, pray tell, or what is he?
Well, if you listen carefully
I'm sure that soon you'll start to see!

The tax-man wasn't one to pray.
He never knew quite what to say.
His tongue got tangled up in knots—
it *would not* speak religious thoughts!

But when a *Pharisee* would pray,
he'd always pray the *proper* way. . .

"I thank you God, as well I ought,"
he'd Phari-say, "that *I am NOT*

a lumpy, grumpy, slimy, sleazy,
smelly, dirty, grimy, greasy,
ooey-gooey, icky-pooey,
fellow through and through and through me!"

"I fast TWO whole times per week.
I'm helpful, friendly, kind, and meek.
But wait, there's more—oh yes, it's true—
I'm modest, pure, and humble, too!"

"Remember, I tithe ten percent
of every cent I ever spent.
Not ten-point-one, or nine-point-three,
but TEN percent—exact-o-ly!"

The Pharisees were quite content.
Their righteousness was evident.
But *tax collectors*, as you'll see,
were nothing like the *Pharisees*.

They taxed for this. They taxed for that.
They taxed you when you tipped your hat.
They taxed you when you blew your nose.
They taxed that stuff between your toes!

They said, *"That's just the way it goes. . ."*

. . .then taxed your Grandma's underclothes!

Now, every tax collector knows

he's *hated* everywhere he goes.

The tax collector never pled.
He never even raised his head.
"Oh God, have mercy. I have sinned."
Yes, that was all the old man said.

"What kind of goofy prayer is that?"
the Pharisee guffawed and spat.

"Oh God, as you can surely see,
THIS *tax-man* here is not like ME.
Yes, I could set THIS fellow straight.
But not right now. It's getting late—
my Bible study starts at eight!"

So off they went along their way.
And God forgave ONE man that day.
ONE MAN went home as white as snow.
But which one? Tell me, do you know?

Now, I *don't* think that God's impressed
by what we say, or how we dress—
or what we do, or did, or don't—
or what we will, or what we won't.

That's *outside* stuff. It's all okay.
It isn't wrong, unless one day
we find we're looking down our nose
and snorting, *"I'm not one of those!"*

For *"one of those"* needs one of YOU
to share the things that GOD can do!

neBUCHaDneZZaR'S CRaZY DReam

Daniel 4

OH, LORD, WHAT A DREAM...

Oh, Lord, what a *dream*—what a *scare*—what a *fright!*
What a white-knuckled, tooth-grinding, *terrible* night!

My taste buds were tingling—my toenails were taut!
My BIG belly-button curled up in a knot!
My tongue twitched and twittered then tangled-up tight.
My eyeballs bugged out with each crazy, new sight!

So I called for my psychics and sayers of sooth,
and I asked them to listen and tell me the truth,
of this verily, scare-ily, raise-up-your-hair-ily,
dream that I dreamt by myself, solitarily!

"Listen King Neb, we've been through this before.
Your dreams are so weird, we can never be sure
if you're seeing the future—it could be, instead,
that you're eating too much spicy food before bed!"

"Too much spicy food? Eating right before bed?
What on earth was I thinking up there in my head?
You really are wise. Please forgive me, " I said.
"Go and get me that new kid—*or you guys are dead!*"

So they went and got Daniel. They brought him upstairs.
They sat him in one of the king's favorite chairs.
They turned and bowed-down 'til their heads touched the ground,
then they shot him their *let's-see-you-do-better* stares!

"Oh, great king," Daniel said, "Spit it out. Go ahead.
What's this heart-thumping , goose-bumping,
dream that you dread?"

"The dreaded, dream fright-mare that's puzzling me,
was a dream of a spreading-wide whopper-sized tree!
It was bigger and better than all of the rest.
It stretched halfway to heaven and blocked out the rest!

And the people, ALL people, looked up to the tree.
It took care of them all quite omnipotently!
And not just the people—the animals too—
every bird, bee, bat, cow, cat and kanga-ma-roo.

And then, just as quick as my dream had begun,
there stood something or some*one* that shined like the sun!
He *reached down* from the heaven—the lights flickered out.
Then that something or *someone*—he started to *shout!*"

"Chop down the tree. Cut it up. Pull it out!
Lop off its branches, stems, twigs, leaves, and sprouts.
Bind up its stump with a chain made of brass.
Surely these things shall ALL come to pass!

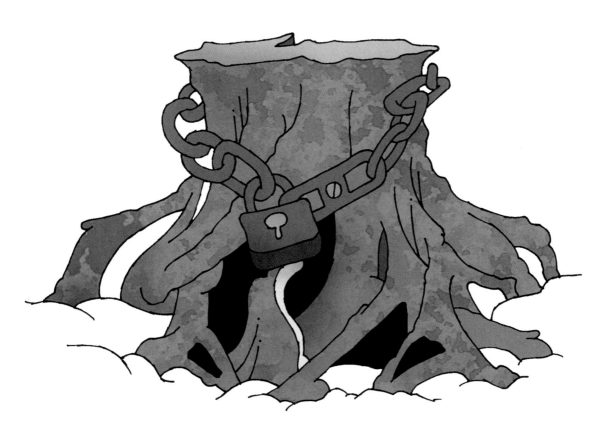

For seven long years let him graze with the cows.
Let him slop with the pigs. Let him grunt with the sows.
Let the dew drench his back and the hair on his head.
Let him know that he knows Who it is who has said,
'The kingdoms are MINE—there is no other one.'

So let it be written. So let it be done!"

Poor Daniel said nothing. His eyeballs popped out.
His jaw hit the floor like a forty-pound trout.

His hair shot straight-up on the top of his head,
for he knew what God meant—
and God meant what He said!

"Umm, Nebuchadnezzar. . . There's one little thing.
Now, how should I put this?" he said to the king.
"That tree that you saw in your dream—well, it's true.
That down-to-the-ground chopped-up tree, King, IS YOU!

God wants you to know, Neb, that HE is the Boss,
and *you* and your whopper-sized pride will be tossed
right-on-out of the kingdom, as quick as a flash.
Unless you repent, it's BOOM!—out with the trash!"

Well, old Neb got the point.
Oh, and wouldn't have you?
So he did what God said. . .

For an hour or two.

"Just look at this place. So majestic. So tall!
Mighty Nebuchadnezzar—the Lord of it ALL!

My gardens are hanging. My stairways climb high.
My BIG-ziggurats stretch straight up to the sky!
It's all so amazing I hardly can speak.
I'm a big Babylonian right at his peak!

Have I squished a few folks? Sure, but what can I say?
This kingdom is mine—and I did it *my way!*

And wouldn't you know it—it happened that fast.
All the things Daniel said—*every one* came to pass!

The people arose. They attacked with a shout.
They moved him on-up, and they threw him on-out.
Nebby moo'd with the cows, just the way that God said,
and he did 'til he finally came to his head.

"Seven long years. Now I finally see.
GOD is the one to be praised—not me!

All those whoopie-ding, I'M-the-king things that I did,
all that look-at-me stuff, oh Lord, heaven forbid
that I ever do any of THAT stuff again.
For You are the King and You always have been!

And not just *a* king, but *the* King of ALL Kings.
The King of all kingdoms and peoples and things!"

And even that man—*even Nebuchadnezzar*—
when he said *"Please forgive me,"* God had the great pleasure—
in the wink of an eye, just as quick as a flash—
of tossing his sins out *for good* with the trash.

There's *never* been *anyone*. . .
There *never* will be—
who GOD can't forgive.
Try it. You'll see!

write to Phil A. Smouse

Once upon a time, Phil A. Smouse wanted to be a scientist.

But scientists don't get wonderful letters and pictures from friends like you. So Phil decided to draw and color instead! He and his wife live in Lancaster Pennsylvania. They have two children they love with all their heart.

Phil loves to tell kids like you all about Jesus. He would love to hear from you today! So get out your markers and crayons and send a letter or a picture to:

phil@philsmouse.com

Or visit his website at http://www.philsmouse.com/

Made in the USA
Monee, IL
11 February 2020